I0087121

Motivation Ignited!
10 Ways to Set Your
Self – Motivation on Fire

By

Dr. Aikyna Finch

Motivation Ignited!

DEDICATION

To all of the people that will be helped by this book:

Thank you for making an investment in yourself and taking your life to the next level! This is an important time in your life because you have made the decision to go for your goals and the first step is Self-Motivation. Remember that your dreams are worth the work and sacrifice, so do not give up on your purpose!

DR. AIKYNA FINCH

Motivation Ignited!

Motivation Ignited!

CONTENTS

Motivation Ignited!

1. MINDSET

The definition of Mindset is an intention or inclination. So to change your mindset is to change your intention or inclination. This is very important to self-motivation because it is the foundation of who you think you should and will be.

My first lesson in mindset was in 2nd grade when I had my first issue with schoolwork. My identity at the time was that I was the smart girl and when I didn't understand the work, it really shocked me. The low of being without your identity is very difficult to anyone let alone a second grader. It is so hard to process that there is a different way in which it can be done and the idea of having to process it so quickly can truly call the block. This is what happens to me when I don't understand; when things don't flow, my mind just stops. It can't move forward until I figure out the issue. I had never experienced this before and did not know how to handle it. The feeling made me feel helpless. It took my teacher to remind me that I was not a failure and I was made for success. She worked with me before and after school to build my skills and confidence in myself. I had to learn that I was not going to be good at everything. I had to shift my mindset to the point where it was okay for me not to be the best as long as I did my best. This was a great lesson that I took throughout my life but it is something I have struggled with throughout my life. Even though I struggle, I have never been defeated and that is the gift that a positive mindset has given me throughout my life.

There is great power in mindset. If you go into a situation defeated, then you will be defeated. But if you go into the same situation believing that you will win, then you will have a better outlook and usually a better outcome. You will be surprised by the number of lives that have been changed by positive mindset. The obstacles that have been overcome by positive mindset will surprise you. You will be surprised by the personal power that has been found because of positive mindset. Mindset is the foundation to igniting your self-motivation. Every structure needs a foundation. Not just any foundation but a strong foundation, a foundation that will not waiver nor break. A lot of structures are built on faulty foundations that eventually come crashing down. When you cut corners in your foundation, you are cutting corners on your full structure. I say this to point out that when you have a negative mindset, then it's very hard to produce a positive product. And when you start out with a positive mindset, it's hard not to produce a positive product. As far as igniting your self-motivation, mindset is the firewood. It's going to be the base of your fire, what is going to hold the fire together. You have to have quality wood in order to get a quality fire. If you come with green wood, you'll get a green fire, but if you come with mature wood, then you are going to get a mature fire. What kind of wood are you using to build your fire? Think about this thought carefully because this is the time to change your wood if you are not coming with the quality. This is where you start to believe in yourself and get ready for the work you are about to do to improve yourself. Make sure that you are ready for the journey, because there are going to be many obstacles along the way—because when you improve yourself, the layers will be pulled back to get to the root of the issues and the layers are going to come with things you may not want to face. It's your mindset that will take you through the journey to the end. Please make sure that your mindset foundation is strong so it will be able to be like the internal flame.

When it comes to self-motivation, mindset is the foundation for greatness. If your mindset is not right, then you are putting your dreams on a shaky foundation. You know what you want and you are ready to put in the work, but you just do not know to do is better than not believing that you are worth the dream coming true. Do you know how many dreams are out there dying daily because of mindset? You have to believe you can make your dreams come true and you are the one to make the dream come to reality. These two things can make or break your success when the going gets rough. This is the importance of mindset and why it is the dream's foundation—because it holds everything together.

As you work on your mindset reflections, remember that once you are solid in your mindset, then you can start uncovering your passion and your purpose. They are related but not the same. You can go through life without ever uncovering them, but that is something that no person should ever feel. You can work on the belief and gratitude; set your intentions and vision boards. Then work on accountability and get a coach so you can get your reward of the greater you!

REFLECTIONS ON MINDSET

Motivation Ignited!

_____

_____

_____

_____

_____

_____

_____

Motivation Ignited!

_____

_____

_____

_____

_____

_____

_____

_____

2. PASSION

The definition of Passion is a strong and barely controllable emotion. It is that feeling when you have to do what your heart is calling you to do in life. Sometimes that thing will evolve as you evolve, but it is usually in the same arena. Your passion will be completely different only when you have not been working on your passion from the beginning.

I've known since I was five years old that I wanted to teach. At 28, I got a taste of my purpose and at 33, I began living in my purpose at the University level. I was a recent doctorate graduate, ready to transition from student to professor in the world of higher education to make a difference in students' lives the way my professors had done in my life.

Being a professor is an honor to me because of the impact that it can have on students and the world. If I do my job in excellence, then I could possibly spark something in my students that will take them to the next level. My goal is for every student that enters my class to leave better than they came. I want to expose them to new thoughts and experiences, and ignite the passion for the subject matter so they will crave more knowledge. Teaching real-world topics and thinking out of the box has always helped me relate to the students on a higher level and allowed me to pour my passion for learning into them.

My supervisor at the time referred me for my current position because my colleagues saw skills in me that would be perfect for the position. At the time, I loved being an onsite dean and was quite successful at that position. While I was ready for a promotion, I never thought it would be in a different department of the university. I had to realize that this promotion was going to expand my skills and stretch my comfort zone for the better. In order to reach your

potential in life, you have to strive for greatness. I did my research on the position and, like the position I had, it involved a new team that was developed to make innovative changes in education.

As I grew older and I experienced new things, my horizons started to broaden. I started to realize that I was good at many different things that I never knew before. I started to lean towards my love of social media and the new component of live streaming. It was out of my comfort zone but it was a great way to spread my message and share my gifts. People started to take notice of my social media and motivation skills, which opened up different opportunities for me. I decided to get a coaching certification to learn about my developing passion and that only accelerated my passion for motivation. Then one day I discovered Periscope and the rest was history. This was the day when my passion for motivation and social media started to coexist. I realized that my message had an audience and a following. I was asked to be a speaker a Periscope Summit and interviewed by numerous shows due to my social media presence. I was asked by many people to share their information with my audience and that is when the influencer and ambassador opportunities came into play. Then the live streaming options started to evolve; I realized that this was something I wanted to be a part of full-time. Eventually, I left Education Administration to pursue my passions through my companies Changing Minds Online LLC and Finch and Associates LLC. I am not for being tied down or transformed by a company that is not my own. I had to realize that my passion included me being free from Corporate America.

Passion in relation to self-motivation is a strong step. The desire to do what you love will take your self-motivation to the next level. When you are doing something that you know is not a fit to your being, then you can feel like you are slowly dying. It can cause illness, depression and more if you are not careful. You will feel a natural pull towards what you are supposed to be doing as time goes on. It will start off small but the pull will grow as time goes on. It is your choice to fight the call but remember that it is never work when you are doing something you enjoy. Sometimes your passion is something easy and sometimes that requires certifications and degrees, but either way, it is worth it because your heart and soul is in it. Do not let anyone down your passion just because they do not understand it. If it is meant for you to do, it will happen, no matter what. So work your plan but know the difference between a season passion and a reason passion. A season passion is something that is hot right now; a reason passion is something that will be there throughout your life. Many people have stepped out on season passions and had to regroup when they found their reason passions.

As you work on your passion reflections,

make sure that you have a strong grasp on your passion and the next best thing does not sway it. Once you have the passion down, then it is time to uncover your purpose.

REFLECTIONS ON PASSION

_____

_____

_____

_____

_____

_____

_____

Motivation Ignited!

_____

_____

_____

_____

_____

_____

_____

Motivation Ignited!

_____

_____

_____

_____

_____

_____

_____

3. PURPOSE

The definition of Purpose is the reason for which something is done or created. It is important to know the reason why you are here and why you do what you do. Taking the time to explore yourself and truly being clear about your purpose is a gamechanger.

Purpose is a very interesting concept. Some people always know their purpose in life. Some people stumble into their purpose and some people will never know their purpose. I have felt like I fell in each of these categories at one point in time. It is amazing how time and life can change your focus when it comes to your purpose. I have known what I was going to do since I was a child but how I accomplish it has totally changed over time.

My purpose began at five years old when I realized that I thought teaching was the best thing in the world. I wanted to be the best teacher in the world. As I got older, I would finish my year work earlier than my classmates and I would be allowed to go to the younger classes and serve as a teacher's aide for the rest of the year. I would grade papers (mostly coloring sheets) and read to the children. That was the best thing to me because I was able to help others. I didn't realize then but that was the start of my servant leadership. As I grew, I would get along with the teachers more than the students so I would learn things that the other students wouldn't because I was always around. Those skills would start to develop my resourcefulness and that would be a trait that would take me far.

During my school career, I was introduced to Engineering because of my Math and Tech skills and I left the path of teaching for awhile. After college, I decided to study Business at CTU and this led me back to teaching because I was informed that I could teach Higher Education if I had a Master's degree. I had only thought about K-12 but

Higher Ed was a new horizon. I didn't teach my first Higher Ed class until after my Doctorate, but I did teach in K-12 and did Adult Professional Development along the way. Once I was in the classroom full-time, I had found my purpose—to teach the masses to reach their potential. Then I got into Higher Ed Administration and it was good for awhile but then I realized I needed to be touching lives in a different way.

It was a decision that happened slowly but one day I wanted to be free. I had gotten a taste of podcasting and social media marketing. The freedom and reach were appealing to me and I started to develop a love for the tech aspect of it. I started to use these skills to educate the masses by letting them know different ways to make their dreams come true. Once I realized that this was a way I could make income, I started to truly consider it as a career. As I starting writing, speaking, and advertising in social media, I knew that Higher Education Administration was no longer for me. I dragged along for almost a year, but then it was time to leave. Now I get to grow into the purpose that I am destined to fulfill.

Purpose is something that everyone has and should fulfill. Some people believe that their purpose should be bigger than it is or they decide not to even pursue the possibilities. We all have free will to live the life that we are purposed to live, but it may not come all at once. The purpose will evolve over time, and the skills that are needed to make it happen will develop along the way. Don't feel discouraged if the progress is slower than you would like because sometimes it takes time to produce greatness.

As you work on your purpose reflections, think about what it is and why you are going to make it a reality. Think about what you have achieved toward the goal and what you can do to get closer to living in your purpose. Finally, think about what it will be like to live in your purpose. Think of the lives that will be touched and the issues that will be changed. These reflections will help to focus on the path to your greater.

REFLECTIONS ON PURPOSE

Motivation Ignited!

_____

_____

_____

_____

_____

_____

_____

_____

Motivation Ignited!

_____

_____

_____

_____

_____

_____

_____

_____

4. BELIEF

The definition of Belief is trust, faith, or confidence in someone or something. It is important to you to believe in yourself before you can expect anyone to believe in you. Don't put a standard on others that you can't uphold yourself.

Sometimes you have to believe in yourself to prove things are possible. There were many times that I didn't believe in myself; even though I had the skills and the knowledge, I didn't believe in myself. I used to believe that there was a person to make it happen. This proved to be a hindrance in my development. I realize that belief plays a major part in what you do. When I became a doctor, the first part of my journey, I truly didn't buy in, but in the second part of my journey I had to fight to become the person I knew I was supposed to be. This was an important development because that's when my belief in myself shifted. I realized that I was worth the fight. I realized that it was their job to throw me off my game, but it was my job to stay in the game. By the time I walked across the stage with my doctoral degree, I was the first person to have ever published in my mentor's 25-year career before I graduated. This showed me that I did have the skills necessary to succeed and I could do anything doubt that my mind to in life. This was when my journey in motivation began. I didn't want anyone to feel like I felt without support, without understanding; I wanted them to know how to build their own self-motivation so they wouldn't have to go through what I went through.

Belief is a powerful tool. It has the power to make or break you. The choice is yours to believe in yourself or not, regardless of what others say. People will try to tear you down, tell you that you are nothing, and kill your self-esteem. It is your decision if you're going to fall or if you are going to stand. You won't have to have resilience, willpower, and self-motivation to help you through the journey but you can make it. You have to realize your worth and refuse to let anyone take it away from you. This is where self-motivation comes into play. You have to realize that no one is responsible for being your cheerleader. No one is responsible for singing your praises. No one is responsible for making you feel like you have worth or value. It is your responsibility to do these things. Stop trying to put the responsibility on others when the responsibility only lies in you. You need to realize that your power is in your belief. And the self-motivation is the director of that power. You have to learn how to use it wisely and strategically. Every day we watch people give away their power. They want to be liked, they want to be loved and they want to be appreciated, by other people. But they should be able to get all of that from themselves. Each time that this happens, that person loses their power and most times they don't even know it.

It is amazing that belief holds such power and energy. It is a catalyst to greatness or defeat. If you believe you can move mountains, you will, but if you don't, you won't. It is as simple as that. To make a dream come true, you first have to believe it can happen and once you believe it can happen, you even have to put some action behind it to make it happen. People with belief and action rule the world, because everything starts with a dream and the belief that you can make it happen.

As you work on your belief reflections, get very acquainted with belief. You will learn how to trust your belief system to know what you should and should not believe in throughout life. You also know when to put action behind your beliefs and when to be still. Trust your instincts and your heart as they will never steer you wrong.

REFLECTIONS ON BELIEF

Motivation Ignited!

_____

_____

_____

_____

_____

_____

_____

_____

Motivation Ignited!

_____

_____

_____

_____

_____

_____

_____

5. GRATITUDE

The definition of Gratitude is the readiness to show appreciation for and to return kindness. Being grateful for all kindness great and small is important because it didn't have to be done. If someone sees something and wants to show you kindness let them as you would like others to let you show them kindness as well.

Gratitude is so important to self-motivation because you have to see and be grateful for where you have come and where you are going. Most people are grateful at the end of the process because they are done and they can celebrate, but you need to be grateful during the process because sometimes that is all you have to hold on to at that moment. People take gratitude for granted because it is usually the last thing on your mind at the time. Gratitude needs to be practiced daily to see life and business in a different light.

I know it is hard to be grateful when you are struggling and going through negative change, but you have to see it as you are being prepared for something greater. We are also programmed to see the negative before the positive in most situations, so we have to shift out mindsets to look for the positives and be grateful for them first.

This is something I had to work on for a long time because I only saw the negative, and when positive things came, I thought it was a fluke. Nothing was ever good enough; it had to be better and greater. I was the child that was always supposed to achieve. I had so many expectations put on me sometimes I felt overwhelmed, but I always pushed through. When I became Dr. Finch, the pressure for me became greater and I was expected to do and know things I had never experienced but I made it work. Sometimes you are given the wisdom as the situation arises and then you take that wisdom with you to the next level, and that is what I did. I learned to network and collaborate with others. I also learned the power of research and becoming an expert in your field. All the time I would let the people know that I appreciated their help and support. I never sent final communication without a thank you or I appreciate you. I wanted people to know that I knew that their gifts were a help to me and I always returned the favor when given the opportunity.

I have to admit that I learned the true meaning of gratitude recently when I changed my life focus to entrepreneurship. Things do not fall the way you want them to; they fall the way life wants it to, and it is not the best feeling when you can't plan the way you want. But at the end of the day, you have to be grateful for the experience and the growth. I do not take things for granted anymore because they do not have to be there. I do not expect things from people because they have shown me who they are and I believe them. I do not hold on to negativity because it gets you nowhere. So, in the end, I realized that gratitude does shift your thinking and it helped in the maturing process as well.

As you work on your gratitude reflections, remember that gratitude should be an everyday practice. Get you a journal or notebook and write down what you are grateful for each day. Then once a month look back on the entries and see the growth that you have made along the way. Notice that your world is not as dark as you may think and that you are moving towards your greater daily. People do not know that you are grateful for them unless you tell them. So send a note or an email and share your gratitude with others.

REFLECTIONS ON GRATITUDE

_____

_____

_____

_____

_____

_____

_____

Motivation Ignited!

6. INTENTIONS

The definition of Intention is an aim or plan. Having a plan for the personal and professional parts of your life will serve as a blueprint but keep it fluid as life can change in a moment and the plan needs to be able to change with it.

Intentions are very important to your self-motivation. They are important because you have to know what you want in life. In order to accomplish a dream, you have to have a dream. People go through life just letting things happen to them and never have a goal.

I have always had dreams but I used to think they would come to me without work. I believed that I was entitled to the best and it would just come. For a while that was the way my life was but when I was 16, my life changed and it has never been the same since. I had a job at the time, so I started to work to support my needs and I realized that

I had a strong work ethic. Work was easy and I started to get attention for my job performance. I started out working to pay for things for school and bills, but then, working became what made me feel important. This became my crutch, and everything else started to fall to the background; it did not make me feel valued. I went on a path to grow in the company and gave up my dreams of being great and became ok with being needed. Then one day I hit a crossroads where my dream of becoming an engineer and my dream of moving up in the company was taken away from me. This was my first experience with the downside of corporate America. But it wouldn't be my last.

Because of that incident, I had to reorder my life and I had to refocus my intentions. I did get a degree from the school of engineering but not the one I wanted, and I am long gone from that company that once was my world. My intentions became educational, and I reached doctoral status, and it did change my life. When I entered the educational world at first, it was new and exciting, but it eventually became the crutch, and I was caught up in the same cycle of the first company that I worked. My need to be important clouded my focus, and I lost my love of teaching and publishing for education. At the end, they got my creativity and drive while I was left drained and used. Some people can just take the hits and keep moving but I am loyal to a fault, and that was a huge betrayal to me and I was done. I had started separating from the company in my heart because I had got a test of entrepreneurship and the world of live streaming, but when I finally separated from the company for good, I gained my life again. I was so wrapped in their culture and beliefs that I lost my own.

The first step to regaining your life is to restate the goal and then you make intentions around the goal. I knew the goal was to build a life where I was helping others reach their greater while I used my gifts to live in my purpose. The goal was easy because that had always been in the core of my heart. The intentions were the hard part. I have always been able to do things I wanted to do that did not require other people but now I was focused on things that totally involved other people, and it was new territory. How was I going to live in my purpose when I had to depend on getting clients and contracts? It was going to be hard because I had to change people's mindset from free content to paid content. What I started to notice is that people put you in categories. They are not willing to pay; they are unwilling to pay for something they think should be free and that was a huge eye opener for me. So my focus shifted because I realized that I had to change mindset before I could be successful or I had to get a whole new audience that came in paying for my content. Both options required work on my part, and I had to decide if I was willing to do the work or go back to corporate America? So what did I decide? I decided that I am an educator and I needed that in my life, so I joined a new university that valued development and entrepreneurship for their people. Then I decided to do the work for my businesses to be successful separately. I decided not to compress my interests but to let them all flow and see how they grow. Entrepreneurs do many things and that is what makes their empires. I decided to create an empire…what about you?

The point of this story is you can have all the intentions in the world but you have to be willing to do the work to make them a reality. Intentions on paper are dreams, but intentions with action are the beginning of greatness. You have to have the mindset and the determination that you will not be moved. You will be tempted and distracted to go in other directions. You will also find yourself along the way if you do the process correctly. You will find that the core never changes—just the path may be different.

As you work on your intentions reflections, realize that you have to have a goal. You have to want to do something with your life. You have to have a purpose. I have been heading for a goal all my life. Sometimes I would reach the finish line and sometimes I would redirect. But I learned to know early which situation is which and start saving time. You will get to that point and you will start knowing what is even worth pursuing in the beginning. Your intentions are your promises to yourself, so they are easy for us to break because we are only disappointing ourselves but what we need to remember is that when we honor our intentions and complete them then we are saying we see the value in ourselves and that is crucial.

REFLECTIONS ON INTENTIONS

Motivation Ignited!

Motivation Ignited!

_____

_____

_____

_____

_____

_____

_____

_____

7. VISION BOARDS

The definition of Vision Boards is a visual representation of your dreams helping you to put your attention on what you want to manifest in your life. Seeing your vision every day is a great way to connect and celebrate with your achievements and your journey.

Vision Boards are an expression of your hopes and dreams in pictures. Creating one can be a very cleansing experience. It is a way to see your life the way you want it to be versus where it is and where it was at one time. Sometimes it is more powerful to see the vision when it is tangible and right in your face. Then you ask yourself the questions like, "Why did I pick the pictures that I chose?" and "Would these pictures be on my board five years from now?" These are just a few questions that flow through your mind as you pour your energy into Vision Board.

There should be a lot of thought put into how you present your hopes and dreams. Will it be in an album, poster board or in a frame? I chose a three-section presentation board. Then I went through dozens of magazines trying to find pictures that will represent my future life. Once all of the pictures are chosen, I then start grouping them into categories according to the goals I want to present on the board. Then it is time for placement; this is where I design the board visually before I put the glue on so I can see if anything is missing or needs to be removed. Once all the pieces are in place now, it is time to glue the vision to the board. As each piece going down the vision is becoming real. You are putting it out into the atmosphere and you are claiming it. This moment for me was a powerful experience because I was taking ownership of everything I was feeling inside that I may or may not say vocally. As I looked at the finished product, I realized that some dreams were easy, some dreams took work and some dreams would never happen. That is the reality of life, but you should always keep faith in the things that you believe in.

It has been my reality that everything I could do alone I was able to conquer but anything that required another person, I do not do so well. As I went through life, I always had time to think about that part later, then one day later showed up. Part of the vision board journey is to put everything there that you want but when you do not accomplish something, it is staring you in the face. It helps you to face the pieces that did not fall the way you wanted them and celebrate the ones that did, and then to find a balance between the two places in life. Part of the lesson is learning that you will not have it all—and it is ok—and that you will still stand in spite of the issue because there is always a plan B. There is healing in that knowledge as well as a sense of maturity that not everyone receives in life. Be glad you are one of the lucky ones that got to have that experience of growth.

As you work on your vision board

reflections, look at your vision board and take in all of the dreams you have in life. Make a plan to work towards each one because every dream deserves some energy. Some will be clear from the beginning, some will start one way and end in another way, and some may remain a dream. In the end, you tried and you do not live your life wondering what could have happened. Go into every dream from a place of YES and you will get outcomes you never imagined.

REFLECTIONS ON VISION BOARDS

Motivation Ignited!

Motivation Ignited!

---

8. ACCOUNTABILITY

The definition of Accountability is the fact or condition of being accountable. It is one thing to want change but it is another thing to take action and be accountable for the change. Being accountable can be self or group driven, know yourself to know what will work for you.

Accountability is a major part to self-motivation because you have to get the dream done. If there is no accountability, then we would make plans and goals but they would never come true. This is also the hardest part of self-motivation because we have to put a value on our dreams. We tend to value others' dreams before our own because we do not want to disappoint others, yet disappointing ourselves never come into play in our minds. Yet if someone else disappoints us, then we are ready to fight. So why do we not fight for our goals?

This was always a big issue for me because I

have inherited a trait from my father where if I do not want to do it, I can't do it, period. I have to do it on my time in my way. I need to see the benefit in doing the task for it to be done quickly. If it is something I can put off, I will. This happened in my education, job, volunteer work and I had intentions to get it done but I did not put any accountability on it because I did not want to, and to this day, some things never got done. I hated disappointing people, so I would take it on, then I would get overwhelmed and I would miss deadlines because I would mentally crash. So how could I fix this problem? Because I did not do this in all areas of my life—just the things I was not interested in doing. I first had to realize that I was not running my own company, so I had to do what people told me to do; this was not going to work long term. Even if I was an entrepreneur, I would have to do things I did not want to do, so I had to get over this trait quickly.

So what did I decide to do, I started holding

myself accountable for the things that were hard for me to perform. I had to start using a calendar and scheduling my time. This became interesting when everything I did had its own calendar; I merged all of my calendars to my Google calendar so I did not overbook. Then I started to pay attention to things that were on my schedule and what I could and could not be a part of in the future. In order to be accountable, you have to know what is going on in your world and not let the world overtake you. Once I realized this nugget, it really helped my brand.

Please pay attention to the things you are involved in because they are shaping your time and your brand. Do not just take on things for visibility that are not aligned with your values and goals. You have to be accountable for the picture you are putting out to the world as well as the amount of information about you. Do not be known as someone that is not on your game and does not give value because people will leave you on the sidelines. You have to be ready to take care of business and show results because people are watching. It is hard when you are first growing and can't afford help but you need to realize that the business will not grow if you do not provide what you promised. This should be a great motivation factor because no one wanted to have a bad brand.

As you work on your accountability reflections, remember that accountability plays a huge part in your life and business. You need to realize how important the goal is, set intentions, and then hold yourself accountable to those intentions. When it is all said and done, you need to see your success as important as your clients' and give yourself the time and energy it takes to make it happen. It is not going to be easy to make the shift but it is worth it because your brand depends on it.

REFLECTIONS ON ACCOUNTABILITY

Motivation Ignited!

_____

_____

_____

_____

_____

_____

_____

_____

9. COACHING

The definition of Coaching is a form of development in which a person called; a coach supports the learner or client in achieving a specific personal or professional goal. When you have made it as far as you can by yourself, get some help to get to your next level.

As a Certified Life Coach, I learned how to ask the open-ended questions to get the Aha moments from my clients. I learned how to tell if there are blocks and how to approach them. Some blocks you have should be hit head on, some blocks need to be dealt with in pieces, while some blocks need to be explored to find the cause. But no matter what type of block it is, it needs to be addressed. This is the goal of coach—to help the client peel back the layers to find what lies underneath. We subconsciously put up walls and layers to protect ourselves but the same walls and layers hinder us from moving to our greater. So this is the time when our crutch becomes our curse and we have to separate from it in order to go to our next step in life. It is so important that we explore coaching in our lives because it is an outlet to get your feelings out, yet see the way life truly is and not what you have made it to be. The coach will guide you in the right direction, but they can't tell you the way to go. The client needs to make their own discovery the discovery what is right for them. They need to take ownership of the decisions that they've made and that they have to make in order to become the person they are destined to be in life. This is where self-motivation comes in again—you have to be motivated in order to go to the process. You have to be motivated to do the work to become the person you're supposed to be. You have to be motivated to do what is necessary to move to the next level. Issues are going to come to play but you have to be steadfast and unmovable when obstacles try to take you off your path.

There comes a time when you have to invest in yourself to move to the next level. You do not have to do it alone but you do have to put in some effort and time. My first investment in myself is when I decided to become Dr. Finch. I had no intention to apply for the doctoral program that day. All I wanted was to take three classes to get my degree in Project Management, but instead I took what I thought was a survey that ended up being an application for the doctoral program. During the program, I received the best training on the necessity of development. One day someone walked in my life that would be one of my best coaches in career and in life. He made me realize the potential of the industry I have loved since I was five years old. Throughout my career in Education, he was there helping and guiding me along the way. There came a time when I did not need him as much professionally but he became one of my best friends instead.

Due to what he did for me, I decided to

become certified as a coach so that I could give back the knowledge and service that was given to me. Part of coaching is the ability to ask the questions that are going to help your client reach their Aha moments to move to the next level. Coaches come to your life for a reason and a season to give you the guidance needed to excel in their area of expertise. It is ok to have several coaches at a time, especially when you are developing the whole person. You have to be ready for the work and you have to be open to change. The coach is going to ask you questions that you may not want to answer and give you assignments that you will not want to do but you have to remember that it is for the development of you. The more outside of the box it is, the more you will step out of your comfort zone and expand your horizons for the better. Always remember that you do not know what you do not know, meaning there is more than what is in your current scope of knowledge.

As you work on your coaching reflections, remember you have to want to reach for the stars at all times. You have to want to be better than you are right now and that is where the coach will come in to help you reach those goals and move into your greatness. The mission is ours to complete but they never said you have to do it alone. Use your coach as a resource to your greatness. Get a plan, do the work and get ready for the reward of the ideal you!

REFLECTIONS ON COACHING

_____

_____

_____

_____

_____

_____

_____

_____

_____

_____

_____

_____

_____

_____

Motivation Ignited!

---

10. REWARD

The definition of Reward is a thing given in recognition of one's service, effort, or achievement. Celebrate all achievements great and small because they all are steps on the journey to the goal. Work without celebration will drain your tank, so fill yourself up by celebrating you.

Reward can be a very strong motivator. It makes people want to go for the gold so they can get the prize at the end of the rainbow. Many people just work for the reward—meaning that they were to see what they could get but sometimes, the reward doesn't match the work that was put in to the project. Sometimes we have to get past what we're going to get out of something and just do it. Not every reward is monetary; some rewards are psychological and some rewards are life changing.

What do I mean by life changing? It is a

lesson that comes from the experience that will bring you a new understanding. As a child, I had three generations in my life and each one of them served their purpose. My Mother was the worker bee. She was the one that made everything happen. I think she was my mindset foundation because if she dreamed it, she wouldn't rest until it became a reality. My Grandmother was the diva. She was beautiful and strong willed. Everything was about her at all times in her world and you better get on board or exit stage left. She was my determination foundation. She knew she was worth everything and more. If she wanted it, that was it; there was only option A, and to this day, I still am that way about many things in my life. My Great-Grandmother was the caregiver. She loved to take care of me. She was my empowerment foundation because she never let me think I was less than greatness. I spent my first three years with her every day all day that my mother forced me to go to head start so I would learn how to deal with children. She knew I was different and she nurtured those things in me and after her, no one truly understood me again.

So what was the life-changing reward? The reward was that I had the honor to have three women in my life that filled my heart, mind and spirit with the tools needed to be the woman that I am today. Because of them, I have the ability to see the potential in others, to go get what I want and know I deserve it. There was a time that I could not make that statement, but over time I reached back to my childhood teachings and realized that I was taught to be strong, willful, mighty, direct and real. I lost that person along the way but she is slowly coming back and she is coming back stronger than ever. Do not get me wrong; I wanted and got the monetary rewards and accolades but as I get older, I realize that it is about the difference you make in the world.

When it comes to the reward of self-motivation, it is the feeling you get when you are at peace with who and what you are in life. You have to realize that no one is obligated to support you or your dreams. If you need that, then there is still work to be done. Pursuing your dreams can be the loneliest place to be at times and you have to be able to stand in spite of the situation. You also have to work for the goal, not just a reward. There have been many times when you put in so much work and all you get is a thank you. You have to be ok with the thank you or don't put yourself in the position for something that you can't handle. It takes great strength to do something and expect nothing in return. That is why we have so many service positions and not enough workers to do the job. Sometimes the reward is giving of yourself, your time and your talents so you can find out what you love and are purposed to do. Make the biggest investment in yourself and reap the reward of your purpose because some people never get that opportunity in life. You have to realize that you are worth the development and the growth that comes with the work. Sometimes that is rewarding enough because you have discovered your true worth. When you look in the mirror and you see the person that has surpassed your wildest dreams staring back at you sometimes is the best reward.

As you work on your reward reflections, remember the moment when you look around and you are living in the dream that you brought to reality after much hard work and sacrifice, then you will know the feeling of the ultimate reward of living your life to the fullest with no apologies!

REFLECTIONS ON REWARD

_____

_____

_____

_____

_____

_____

_____

_____

_____

_____

_____

_____

_____

_____

_____

Motivation Ignited!

_____

_____

_____

_____

_____

_____

_____

_____

CONCLUSION

There are so many ways to become motivated. You can be motivated by people, places, causes, and the list goes on. People are drawn in and motivated by different things and different ways. The goal is to be able to be motivated by your goals and dreams. Self-Motivation comes easy for some and hard for others, but at the end of the day, you need to find out how it works for you. Some people have the best intentions but if someone is not in the background pushing them along, then nothing will get done. Then there are others that go, go, go until they shut down and they don't need anyone to get them moving. There are also people that fall in between the two spectrums, but you need to know where you fall so you can decide where you want to be and do the work.

There are so many reasons why we need to ignite our self-motivation. There are going to be times when people are not going to understand the vision and you will have to stand-alone. There will be times when you have to make decisions that others do not understand. There are going to be times when you have no support system to depend on and these are the times when you have to lean on your own self-motivation. We have to be able to go to the next level when the world is there and when there is no one there. We have to know that we are worth all the dreams that we have for our lives. We have to know that our worth is not determined by man but by something so much higher. If you were born, then you have a purpose in life and no one can take it away from you. There is a fire within you to bring this purpose to reality and only you can stop it from happening because you put it on the backburner for and because of others.

Do you ever ask the question, "When is it my time?" Is the answer always later? When will the answer be...now? There comes a point when the answer is Now because tomorrow is not promised and you do not want to spend your life saying, "Woulda, Coulda, Shoulda!" It is time to take a stand for your best resource…You! Why is everyone and everything more important than your dreams and goals? Why are you giving your power away instead of standing in it? These are all questions that I have asked myself and people have asked me in my life. They are direct and powerful questions that take you out of your comfort zone. People get complacent with day-to-day life and they stop reflecting over their lives and stop trying to make it to the next level. Sometimes it feels easier to conform to the ways of the world than to fight for your dreams but at the end of the day, aren't your dreams worth the fight?

ABOUT THE AUTHOR

Dr. Aikyna D. Finch is an educator and author. Her teaching includes business, leadership, marketing, social media and information systems at the graduate and undergraduate levels. Dr. Finch has several publications in business and education.

Dr. Finch is the co-author of eight books. She is also a contributor for the Huffington Post and many more.

Dr. Finch is also a certified coach, women empowerment podcaster, speaker and social media consultant/trainer. She coaches in the areas of empowerment, life and social media for individuals and groups. She is the co-host of the Motivate Social Podcast and the Motivation Station Radio Show. She is the Visionary for the Social Power Summit. She is a speaker on the topics of motivation, education and social media. She can be found at @dradfinch on all social media platforms.

For more information about the author, visit:
Personal website: https://aikynafinch.com
Business website: https://technicallyintuitive.com
Show website: https://changingmindsonline.com
Summit website: http://socialpowersummit.com

Motivation Ignited!

www.ingramcontent.com/pod-product-compliance
Lightning Source LLC
Chambersburg PA
CBHW071418040426
42445CB00012BA/1206